· T R O P H I E S ·

BRIGHT SURPRISES

Harcourt

Orlando   Boston   Dallas   Chicago   San Diego

Visit *The Learning Site!*

www.harcourtschool.com

Illustration Credits

Page: 93, 197, Sarah Beise; 141, 213, Carly Castillon; 173, 229, Hugo Cruz; 13, 29, 125, Susan Miller; 69, 85, Jennifer Rarey.

Printed in the United States of America

ISBN 0-15-325340-1

1 2 3 4 5 6 7 8 9 10   039   10 09 08 07 06 05 04 03 02 01

CONTENTS

Dan and Fran 6
by Susan McCloskey

Teacher Read-Aloud Limericks for Laughing . 13

Miss Mack's Tricks 14
by Maria Santos

The Case of the Missing Letter . 22
by Ben Farrell

Teacher Read-Aloud Who Knows? 29

Just a Little Practice 30
by Ben Farrell

You Are in the Olympics! 38
by Jared Jansen

The Race to the Sea 46
by Kaye Gager

Help on the Trail 54
by Robert Newell

Creature Clicks 62
by Kana Riley

Teacher Read-Aloud Have You Read . . . ? . . 69

The Dinosaurs' Brunch 70
by Deborah Eaton

A Special Pup 78
by Nelson Morales

Teacher Read-Aloud The Flea's Wish 85

A New Best Friend **86**
by Sharon Fear

`Teacher Read-Aloud` Is It? **93**

Star Time **94**
by Sydnie Meltzer Kleinhenz

Coach Ben **102**
by Anthony Carmendolla

Room to Share **110**
by Julio Mendez

The Lazy Horse **118**
by Celeste Albright

`Teacher Read-Aloud` You Don't Mean It! . . **125**

The Bravest Soldier **126**
by Glen Harlan

Many Moons Ago **134**
by Diane Hoyt-Goldsmith

`Teacher Read-Aloud` Your Answer, Please! . **141**

Grandpa Tells Why **142**
by Ann W. Phillips

The Snow Baby **150**
by Robert Newell

Good Advice **158**
by Meish Goldish

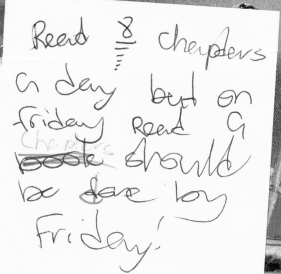

Read 8 chapters a day but on friday Read 9 ~~Chapters~~ ~~book~~ should be ~~done~~ by Friday!

Auction Day . . . .
by Carol Storment

Teacher Read-Aloud Just Horsing A...

A Cookie for the Cowboy
by Caren B. Stelson

How Grandmama Tamed the West . . . .
by Celeste Albright

Harvest Time 190
by Sydnie Meltzer Kleinhenz

Teacher Read-Aloud On the Farm 197

Penny Savers 198
by Meish Goldish

Book of Days 206
by Deborah Akers

Teacher Read-Aloud Summer's Too Short . 213

The Hummingbird Garden 214
by José Gonzales

A Mountain Blows Its Top 222
by Kana Riley

Teacher Read-Aloud Tongue Tanglers . . . 229

The Place in Space 230
by Susan M. Fisher

A Meteor Stopped Here 238
by Kana Riley

Dan and Fran

written by
Susan McCloskey

illustrated by
Mark Bixby

Dan Craft was sad.

"Letters, letters!" he said. "Look at all the letters! Letters for Alf Sands at the police department. Letters for the students in Ann Grant's class. Who will get the letters out?"

"Not Nan. She has to stamp the letters. Not Hank. He has to pack the letters in bags. Not Brad. He had an accident. He fell flat on his back. He was so mad!"

"This is bad!" said Dan. "We are in a jam!"

Then Dan noticed Fran. His expression went from sad to glad.

"Fran!" he said. "You are the one for this task! Here is the plan. Grab the letters. Get them out as fast as you can!"

Fran likes Dan. She obeys all his commands. So Fran did grab the letters. Away she ran.

Cam's dad was glad to see Fran. So were Sal and her pals, Pat and Al. So were Jan and Scamp.

Alf Sands at the police department had his letters in a snap.

So did the students in Ann Grant's class. They were so glad to see Fran hand out the letters. They sang out, "You are grand, Fran! Can you come back?"

So Fran went back with Dan.

Ann Grant's students clapped and clapped.
What an audience!

"Speech, speech!" they said.

They got a speech from Dan, not from Fran.
Her expression said how glad she was. The
audience was glad, too. And so was Dan Craft!

Think About It

1. How do the letters get sent out?

2. Why does Fran not make a speech?

3. Suppose the TV news wants a story about Fran. Write the a sentence to help them.

Limericks for Laughing

A camel with humps on its back
Tried to carry the mail in a sack.
The desert was bumpy,
The camel was lumpy,
And the sack hit the sand with a whack!

I once saw a man with a cat,
Which, in turn, had a little pet rat.
The rat had a flea
That was tickling its knee.
Now what do you think about that?

Miss Mack's Tricks

by Maria Santos
illustrated by Steve Haskamp

"Who is this big, pink pig?" said Nick.

"This is Miss Mack," said Kim. "I am teaching her tricks. Look at this."

Kim said softly, "Sit down. Sit down." She said it twice. Miss Mack did not sit.

"Miss Mack is stubborn," said Kim with a grumble. "She will not listen when I speak."

"It's because you mumbled," said Nick. "Speak to her firmly. Then she will listen."

Nick said firmly, "Sit down! Sit down!" He said it twice. Miss Mack did not listen.

Jill came skipping up to Kim and Nick.

Kim said, "I am teaching Miss Mack tricks. She is stubborn. She will not listen."

"Are you teaching Miss Mack in kid language?" said Jill.

"That is the language I speak," said Kim with surprise.

"I will try," said Jill. To Miss Mack she said, "Sit down!" Miss Mack sat!

"Stand up!" said Jill firmly. Did Miss Mack stand up? She did!

Kim exploded! "Why did my pig listen to you?" she said to Jill.

Jill said, "I can speak pig language."

Then Kim was sad. "I wish I could speak pig language. I want to teach my pig tricks," she said.

"I will teach you," said Jill. "It's like kid language. You just speak with hands, too."

The kids were teaching Miss Mack every day. Now she could do tricks! She could sit. She could sniff. She could zip here and there.

The twins, Tim and Jim, came up. They had their black cat, Ink. Ink did not like Miss Mack!

"Hiss!" said Ink.

"Yip!" said Miss Mack.

Zip! Ink darted off like a black streak.

"Ink! Look out!" said Tim.

"Ink! Come back!" said Jim.

Kim said to Miss Mack, "Grab Ink!" She used her hands.

Zip! Miss Mack darted off to grab Ink. Zip! Miss Mack was back with Ink.

Tim and Jim were glad to have Ink back. Kim was glad that Miss Mack could do tricks!

Think About It

1. What happens when Kim tells Miss Mack to do a trick?

2. How do you think Jill learned to use "pig language"?

3. After Miss Mack saves Ink, the two become friends. Write your idea for an adventure they might have together.

The Case of the Missing Letter

by Ben Farrell   **illustrated by Brian Fujimori**

"Are you Detective Tom?" Min said.

"I am," said Tom. "What can I do for you?"

"I have to find a missing letter," Min said. "It was supposed to go to my mom, but she didn't get it."

"How can you be positive this specific letter to your mom is missing?" said Tom.

"There were two letters for my mom," said Min. "I definitely slid them into the letterbox. She got one, but she didn't get two. Now, that was strange."

"I think I can solve your case," Tom said. You can be my assistant. We'll go to the letterbox to find information. We can't solve this case with no information."

Min and Tom went to the letterbox. Tom saw something strange. "Now, that makes me think," he said.

"What is it?" Min said.

"This letterbox is very full," Tom said. "Maybe some letters fell out."

"Are you positive?" said Min.

"No," said Tom, "but here comes Mr. Bond," Tom said. "We can talk with him."

Mr. Bond had no information. "Some letters did drop out of the box," he said. "I think I got them all." Then Mr. Bond got back to his job.

Tom got down by the box to have a look. He saw something strange. The grass was wet!

Then he said, "Look at this! Is it the stamp that was on your letter?"

Min got down on the grass. The stamp did look like the one on her letter. "I'm not positive, but I think it could be," she said.

"I think your case is solved," said Tom.

"How could it be solved?" Min said. "We didn't find the letter."

"No, but it will find you," Tom said. "We will look in your box. A letter that has no stamp gets returned."

Min ran to her box. There was the letter! "Tom, you are some detective!" she said. "I am glad you could solve this case for me."

"I am glad I could help," said Tom.

Think About It

1. Why didn't Min's mother get the second letter?

2. Do you think Tom is a good detective? Explain.

3. What do you think the missing letter said? Write the letter you imagine Min wrote to her mother.

Who Knows?

What did the log become when it was put on the fire?

What grows shorter as it grows older?

What diamond is the biggest of all?

What should a farmer raise in wet weather?

What kind of dog has no tail?

Answers: hot; a candle; a baseball diamond; an umbrella; a hot dog

Just a Little Practice

by Ben Farrell
illustrated by Jennifer Beck Harris

Ted went to the playground. He had his red
basketball. When he got there, he noticed Pat.
She had her basketball, too. She was getting set.

Ted pretended not to look. Then Pat's basketball
went up. It fell into the net. Ted looked at his
basketball. "Now you go in," he said to it.

As Ted aimed, Pat noticed him. He looked
familiar to her. "Who is he?" she said.

Ted's basketball went up and missed.
Ted ran for his ball. He noticed that Pat was
looking at him. Was she looking when he
missed? Did she laugh when his ball missed
the net?

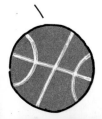

Pat did not laugh. She could see that he
was Ted Wick. His dad, Jack Wick, was a
professional. He was a captain in the NBA.
Jack Wick was one of the best.

"Ted," she yelled at him, "I'm Pat. Let's test
that basketball!"

Ted passed his red ball to Pat. "It was a
gift from my dad," he said.

Pat passed her basketball to him. Then she aimed the red ball. It went up and in! Ted applauded.

"Now you drop one in," Pat said.

Ted aimed Pat's basketball. The ball went up. It hit the back and fell out.

"I can not get one in," Ted said.

Pat had to laugh. "Two misses are not a lot," she said.

"Do not laugh," Ted said. "My dad is coming to the playground. He has to see me make a basket. I can tell that I will not make one."

"You will," Pat said. "I'll be the teacher. It will be my job to help you make one. You are going to get the ball in the basket."

Ted missed and missed.

Then Ted got one in. Pat applauded. "See that!" she said. "You did it!"

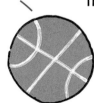

Then Ted asked, "So, can we be friends?"

"We are friends," said Pat.

"Like best friends," big Jack Wick said.

"Dad!" Ted said. "I did not see you come to the playground!"

"The playground monitor let me in. I noticed
what was happening," Ted's dad said. "I let the
teacher do her job."

Pat looked sad. "His teacher can't dribble,"
she said.

"Then let's make a trade," Ted's dad said.
"Now I'll be the teacher."

Pat looked up at big Jack Wick and laughed.

She said, "That's the best trade yet!"

Think About It

1. How does Ted find out how to get the ball into the basket?

2. Why does Jack Wick let Pat teach Ted?

3. Think about the ending of "Just a Little Practice." What do you think happened next? Write the next part of the story. Draw a picture to go with it.

YOU ARE IN THE OLYMPICS!

by Jared Jansen
illustrated by Larry Day

An ancient stadium is host to the Olympics this year. You are an athlete, here for the running competition.

The first day, you parade with the athletes into the stadium. You think of your mom and dad. They are there in the stands. They like all sports competitions. The Olympics will be fun for them.

In the stadium, you listen to a speech. It makes you think. Then the athletes parade out of the stadium. You cannot see your mom and dad, but you know they can see you.

You will not compete today, but you cannot rest. You must run every day to be fit.

You talk with some athletes as you jog.
Some of them have run in Olympic sports
competitions. Some have earned medals, and
one has set a record. You look up to them.

You listen as they trade information and
running tips. They cannot forget the big day
that is coming! They speak of how they want to
perform in the competition. These are the top
athletes. Will you be one, too?

Your mom and dad come to see you. They laugh as they talk of the fun they have had. You tell them of the top athletes you have met.

Then your mom and dad have to go. The sun is going down, and you must get to bed. You have to be rested for your big run the next day. You go into your hut and hop into bed.

When the athletes get up, they must be fed.
Everyone gets on the bus to go for something.
You have eggs, milk, and a bun. You must be
strong for running.

Back on the bus, the athletes who are
running today speak of winning medals. They
all want to get one, but not everyone will.
Will you?

You go to the stadium early and jog a bit. You are ready for a perfect run. You will get out there and go for it!

You get set and you listen for the gun. The run is on! You start well, but will you win?

Your run is not perfect, but you give it your best. Then the run is over. You led, but did you win? You look up. Yes, you did!

When the running competitions are over, the
medal ceremonies are held. Your mom and dad
will see you get the gold!

At last your name is called, and the medal
is yours. Everyone claps and shouts. You are a
top athlete now! You performed well in the
Olympics. Now you can just have fun!

Think About It

1. How does the race turn out?

2. How do you think the girl's parents feel about her being in the Olympics? How do you know?

3. Write about why you would or would not like to perform in the Olympics.

THE RACE TO THE SEA

Story by Kaye Gager

Illustrations by Donna Delich

The beach has a secret. Mom said so.
I look and look for the secret. I look in
a wet log. I get up on a big rock. I am
eager to see the secret. What can it be?

I wish I could dig for it. Mom said no digging at all. That could be bad.

Mom said we can collect litter. I find weird junk, but I do not find the secret. I run down to the big rock. The red sun sets over the sea. We will have to look tomorrow.

The sun is setting when I run down to the beach. Mom runs with me. When we get there, there are fishing ships dancing on the sea. But what is the secret?

Mom gets up on the big rock. I get up with her. We are eager, but we have to sit patiently.

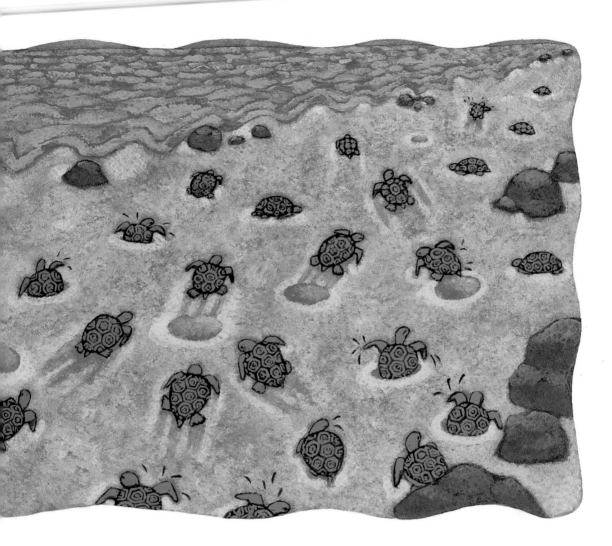

Then I see something. I see something digging! Then I see digging all over the beach.

There they are! Is this the secret? My mom nods. They look weird. Sand is all over them. What are they going to do?

Then they run. Look at that speed! They run for the sea. It looks as if they have trained for it. Are they going to make it?

No! Look up there! A sea gull is going to get one of them! It misses. Mom and I clap and clap.

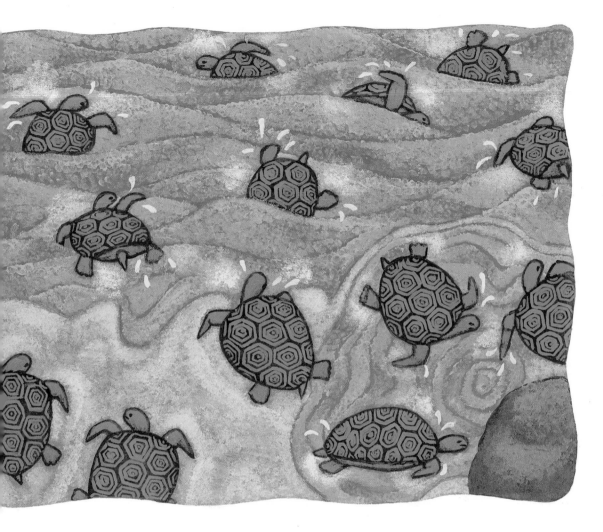

"Come on!" I yell to them. "You have to get to the sea!" They run down the beach to the rocks. The sea gives them a bath. The sand comes off them as they swim. Then the little swimmers go out to sea.

They are like friends now! I will be sad not to see them at the beach tomorrow.

What are they going to do now? That is a secret of the wise sea. I wish I could get a message to them.

I look at the sea and wish them well. The sea gulls can not find them now. My little friends are dancing in the sea. They are swimming in the sun. The sea gulls will have to have fish!

Think About It

1. What secret does the beach have?

2. Why do you think the boy's mom does not tell him what the secret is?

3. Make a postcard from the boy in the story to a friend. Draw a picture on one side to show the secret. Write a message on the other side that tells about it.

Help on the Trail

by **Robert Newell**
illustrated by **Mike Harper**

A chill wind whips the branches. A storm is coming. Mrs. Hatch's husband, Frank, is out hunting. Brandon, who is 12, is with him. She wishes she could telegraph them to come back.

The temperature drops. A bad snowstorm starts. The wind makes the snow hit hard, like splinters.

Are Frank and Brandon lost? They could freeze out there! Did they go north from the ranch or south? Mrs. Hatch can't tell which, but some dogs can.

How do dogs find someone who is lost? They sniff something that belongs to him or her. Then they sniff along the trail, looking for that smell.

Which dogs can do this? Smart dogs. Strong dogs. They have to like adults and children. And they have to have a teacher.

Dogs like this do not just sit and fetch. Starting as pups, they hunt for the teacher over and over.

When someone is lost, dogs like Champ and Patches start sniffing. They are hunting for his or her smell. A snowstorm can't stop them from doing the job. They will find the trail.

This dog stops and barks. It's a signal that he sees someone. ▶

◀ The drifts of snow are up to this dog's chin. She has to inch along. But just watch—she'll get there!

Patches has a red cross strapped to his back. He has a bell on his neck. The bell signals that help is coming. ▶

Help did get to Frank and Brandon Hatch. Some dogs started out at the ranch. They hunted to the north and to the south. They guided friends to the Hatches. Frank and Brandon had gotten lost. They got chilled, but they did not freeze in the storm.

Frank said, "Thanks so much!" What did Brandon do? He had big, big hugs for the dogs!

Think About It

1. How do Frank and Brandon Hatch get back home?

2. Why would dogs be good at finding someone who is lost?

3. What do you think Brandon told his class about being lost in the snowstorm? Write Brandon's story.

CREATURE CLICKS

by Kana Riley

All children like to watch creatures. Some adults do this as a job. They get photos that let us see how creatures survive.

Getting the photos can be hard for them. It has to be something they like to do. Just look at some of the spots they had to go to!

Marine Creatures

This sub went far down in the sea to get this shot. It is so dark that this part of the sea looks black.

Without the sun, some marine creatures still survive. Fish and crabs like the sea bottom.

The creatures there are odd. Notice how delicate some look. This spot could kill us, yet they dart and swim there without harm.

Yard Creatures

You may not have noticed some of the bugs in the yard and in the park. Are you curious? Look at what is out there!

This smart bug looks like an ant. Some friends with feathers can not tell the two apart. They do not like an ant for a snack. So they do not harm this bug. It can survive well in the yard.

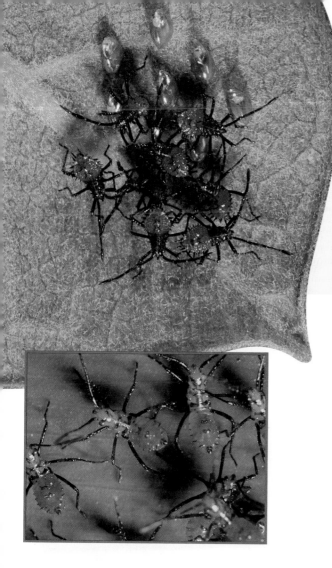

Some mom bugs park next to eggs to see them hatch. Some moms are not curious. They go off to do what they like.

This dad bug has all the eggs stuck on his back. So far he has not collapsed! It can be hard to be a bug!

Think About It

1. Where and how do the creatures in this selection live and survive?

2. How do the photos help you learn about creatures you may not have seen on your own?

3. If you could be any creature you liked, what would you choose to be? Write a paragraph explaining your choice and telling what life would be like as that creature.

Have You Read . . .?

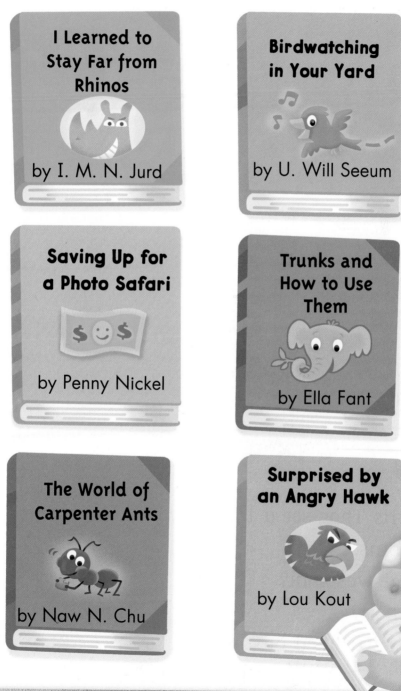

I Learned to Stay Far from Rhinos

by I. M. N. Jurd

Birdwatching in Your Yard

by U. Will Seeum

Saving Up for a Photo Safari

by Penny Nickel

Trunks and How to Use Them

by Ella Fant

The World of Carpenter Ants

by Naw N. Chu

Surprised by an Angry Hawk

by Lou Kout

The DINOSAURS' BRUNCh

by Deborah Eaton
illustrated by Chris Lensch

Morris Thor set a trap. It was all sticks and thorns.

What was that?

A snort?

Morris yanked on the cord.

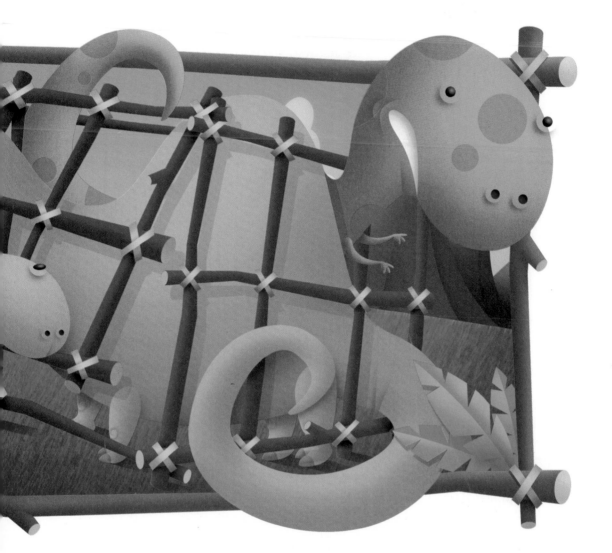

"ROAR!" "ROAR!"

Morris had trapped two dinosaurs! Two
was enough. More than enough! The trap
was crowded. More than crowded! One was
as big as two horses. And that was the
short one!

"ROAR!" One roar was like storms storming.
"ROAR!" One roar was like lava erupting.
The dinosaurs tore at the trap.
Morris's twin, Doris, ran for safety.
"Dinosaurs!" she yelled. "Run, Morris!"

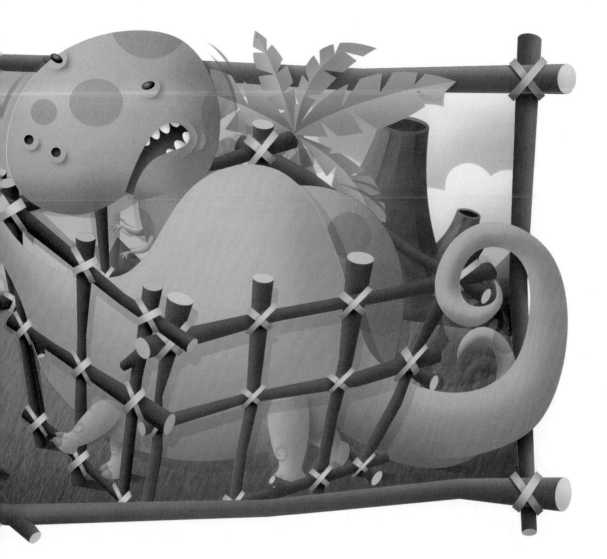

"No," said Morris. "I set the trap, and now I have two big pets."

"Morris," said Doris, "the dinosaurs you trapped are not peaceful ones. They do not like plants. What if they escape? Think what they will have for brunch. YOU on a fork!"

"ROAR!" "ROAR!"

Morris looked at the trap. The top part
was torn.

"They do look sort of mad," he said. "Well,
I have a chore to do."

Morris ran to the egg store. He looked at
all the eggs. "This is not enough," he said.
"Do you have more?"

Then Morris mixed and poured. He had to be quick. The trap was getting worn out.

"Come and get it!" Morris said. He had brunch for the dinosaurs—a big omelet and two corn muffins.

"ROAR!" "ROAR!"

Gobble, gobble, gobble.

They liked it!

"Mmm!" the short dinosaur said. "MORE!"
He looked at Morris. He licked his lips.
Morris yelled, "Doris! HELP!"
Off he ran.

"What is his problem?" the short dinosaur
asked. "I was just going to ask if he could
make apple dumplings."

"He's going to get help," Stretch said. "What
do you think we will have for brunch tomorrow?"

Think About It

1. What happens after Morris sets his trap? What does he plan to do?

2. Why does Morris run off when the dinosaur licks his lips?

3. What do you think will happen tomorrow? What will the dinosaurs do? What will Morris and Doris do? Write about your ideas and draw a picture.

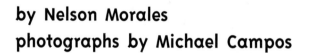

A Special PUP

by Nelson Morales
photographs by Michael Campos

Here I am with our special pup, Flash. That's my sister Sharon on the bench.

Flash is Sharon's dog for now. Mom, Dad, and I all play with him and have lots of fun with him. We work hard on his training, too.

Flash is going to be a working dog. He will help someone who can't see.

Flash will be a good working dog. He is very gentle. He likes everyone, and he can cheer anyone up! He is very smart, too. After his training, he will have lots of important skills for his work.

Sharon and Flash are part of a special program. In this program, kids help train working dogs. When the training is over, Sharon will have to give Flash up. That will be hard for all of us. Still, knowing that he is helping someone will cheer us up.

Flash will have to be comfortable about going anywhere. That's why Mom and Dad take him to work now and then. We also take him to shops and parks. He comes with me when I have an appointment with the doctor. It's part of his training.

Flash likes to go on car trips. He likes to go on the bus, too. All these trips will help him know how to be a good working dog.

Dad and I like to watch big jets come in and land. Flash comes with us. He sits still and watches them with us. I wish I could know what he's thinking!

Mom, Dad, Sharon, and I will go on a jet to visit my grandma. Flash will come with us. That trip will be one of the best parts of training him.

One day Sharon let flash come to class with me. She had to tell me what to do. "One skill Flash has to have is to be still when someone approaches him. Be firm and confident when you tell him what to do. Do not forget to let him know when he is doing a good job."

Sharon had a lot to say! At last, Flash and I were off.

When we got there, Flash and I went into the playground. Lots of kids were playing on the equipment. They jumped down and rushed over to see Flash.

To some of the kids, I said, "Do not approach Flash too fast. Do not yell at him."

To some I said, "It's all right. Flash is very gentle."

Flash let all the kids pet him. "Good dog, Flash," I said.

Flash's training is going well. Maybe I will be the next one to have a special pup like Flash.

Think About It

1. Why does Sharon work hard to train Flash?
2. Why is going everywhere with the family part of Flash's training?
3. If Sharon let Flash go to class with you, what would you do? Make a plan for the day. Tell why you would do each thing.

The Flea's Wish

How I wish the world could see
What fun it is to be a flea!
We jump, we hop, we dance around
Playing games on chow and hound.

Poodle, pointer, pug, and beagle
Think we should be made illegal.
Once a very rude retriever
Told us to hop off and leave her.

Collie, spaniel, spitz, and setter
All believe it would be better
If we fleas would only scat
And go to live on
someone's cat.

A NEW BEST FRIEND

Written by Sharon Fear
Illustrated by Jill Banashek

"Write to me!" Howard shouted.

"I will!" Rick shouted back. The car and the moving van started off. They went down the block, around the playground, and beyond it.

Rick was moving to a new town.

"I wish I could go, too," Howard said to his friend Beth.

"Will you be lonely without him?" asked Beth.

"He was my BEST friend," Howard said seriously.

"Help me with my kite," said Beth. Howard held the kite. Beth unwound some string. She fastened the string to the kite.

"You can get a new best friend," said Beth. Howard frowned. "How? Who?"

Howard's dog bounded up to them. Beth picked up a stick and tossed it. "Get it, Bow Wow!" Beth shouted.

"How about Jack?" she asked.

"Jack does not like Bow Wow," Howard said.

"How about Norman?" said Beth.

"Norman who?" asked Howard.

"His dad has a brown mustache," said Beth.

"Bow Wow does not like Norman," said Howard. "He has a collection of cats."

Bow Wow growled.

Howard picked up his basketball, dribbled it, and shot. It rimmed around and fell out. He passed it to Beth. She dribbled around him. She shot. Pow! She sank it!

"Wow!" shouted Howard. "Outstanding!"

"I have a secret gift," teased Beth. They played on, trading shots.

"Chuck!" she said. "Chuck could be your new best friend."

Howard frowned. "Chuck can't play basketball," he said. "Not like you."

"How about Ben?" said Beth.

"Can't swim," said Howard.

"Patrick?" said Beth.

"Can't play chess," said Howard.

"Carl!" shouted Beth.

"Can't do a cartwheel," said Howard.

"I give up," said Beth, doing a cartwheel.

Then it came to him. Beth was his friend. She was a girl, but she was the best.

"How about you?" Howard said.

She looked at him. "Can you dribble with your left hand?" she teased again.

"Yes," said Howard.

"You wish!" She laughed out loud. "Well, let's work on it now." She passed him the basketball.

"Outstanding!" said Howard.

Think About It

1. Why is Howard looking for a new best friend? Who will be his best friend now?

2. Why does it take Howard so long to know who his new best friend will be?

3. Howard is going to write to Rick. What do you think he will say? Write a letter for Howard to send.

Is It?

If a duck is playing basketball and bumps into another player, is that a fowl foul?

If your dog pants once and then does it again, is that a pair of pants?

If a rabbit goes to the barber, does he ask for a new harestyle?

If you dump a sack of flour onto your pillow, have you made a flour bed?

If you cry because your toes hurt, is that a foot bawl?

story by
Sydnie Meltzer Kleinhenz

illustrated by **Joe Cepeda**

STAR TIME

Mom and Dad,

Help! Camp could not be worse! I went to my first Stars class. I had my star chart. I wanted to look up at the stars. Do you know what? Stars is for campers who want to <u>be</u> stars. It's not for campers who want to <u>see</u> stars! We all have to perform in a talent show. I prefer watching to acting. I want to quit. Come get me!

Forget it. You'll get this letter after the talent show is over. I'll think of something.

I miss you,
Kirsten

94

Kirsten could see Karen and Robert recite lines from a play. Carmen and a girl from cabin 2B did handstands. Josh played the camp song on his horn. Jennifer twirled in her costume. Ernest was making up a poem about bugs.

Kirsten sat alone. She looked at her letter. She looked at the river far away. What was she going to do? She roamed around the camp. Then she went back to her cabin to get her gym bag.

At dusk, Kirsten saw Gilbert. "I do not know what to do for the talent show," he said. "I can't act or make up a poem. I do not know any tricks." He kicked the dirt and hollered, "GROWL!"

"Wow! That was as loud as a dragon," said Kirsten.

"That is my one talent," said Gilbert frowning. "I can be loud."

Kirsten clapped. "I know what we can do!"

Kirsten got her star charts and lantern out of her gym bag. "There are billions of stars," she said. "Some make patterns of things. Look at this."

She stuck a pin into different spots on a card. She put the card over her lantern. It flashed the pattern of stars on a big rock. "Take the lantern. Now do your dragon growl."

Gilbert growled. Kirsten went to the rock and showed Gilbert the pattern in the stars. "Here's the Dragon," she said.

Gilbert and Kirsten got a long, black cloth from the camp director. They pinned it up at the front of the Stars platform. Gilbert helped Kirsten cut spots out of the cloth.

They were all grins when it was their turn at the talent show. Kirsten held her gym bag of props. Gilbert held a funnel to his mouth. They went to the back of the cloth. The campers looked puzzled.

Kirsten flashed her lantern on the back of the cloth. She said, "These are the Big Dipper and the Little Dipper." Gilbert made the sound of dripping water.

For Pegasus, Gilbert made the sound of wings flapping. For the Archer, he made the ping of the string. For the Twins, he made baby sounds. They ended the show with Gilbert's loud growl for the Dragon. The campers clapped and clapped.

Mom and Dad,

Camp is better now! I was in the talent show with my pal, Gilbert. We got to <u>be</u> stars and <u>see</u> stars. Lots of campers are enjoying making star cards for their lanterns. Now we have a new and different Stars class.

Forget about my wanting to quit. I'm having fun!

Love,
Kirsten

Think About It

1. What is Kirsten's problem? How does she fix it?

2. What gives Kirsten an idea for something to do in the talent show?

3. Make a poster for the Stars talent show. Use words and pictures to tell about the show.

Coach Ben

written by **Anthony Carmendolla**
illustrated by **Jeff Shelley**

It was a summer camp ball game in June. The Reds were playing the Tans. The Reds were up in the top of the last inning. The score was Tans 3, Reds 2. With two outs, the bases were filled with Reds.

Up to then, Jeff had been pitching well for the Tans. Now he looked sad. Ben ran over from first base. Tim came out from in back of home plate.

"Cheer up," Ben said. "One out wins the game."

"Yes, and one hit puts the Reds on top," Tim added.

"They may bunt," Jeff said. "They can see that I'm no ballhawk. They just may want to settle for a tie for now."

"Jeff," Ben said, "depend on Tim and me to look out for bunts. You concentrate on pitching."

"Play ball!" the ump yelled.

"All right," Ben said. "Let's see that they don't score."

Jeff looked at the Red player who was up to bat. Was he going to bunt for a tie? Jeff could not know. He got set and pitched.

This batter was not bunting. He let the pitch go by for a ball. He did not swing at all.

"Let him hit!" Ben hollered. "We'll get him out!"

Jeff pitched his best pitch. The Red player's hit was a pop-up.

"I hope Ben can catch it," Jeff said.

Ben ran back, but the pop-up fell in. The Red players were running. As Ben ran for the ball, two of them came home to score. When Ben got the ball in to Tim, the Reds were up by one run.

Ben came over to Jeff. "That missed catch was my fault," he said. "We can still make it up. One out, and we get to bat."

"I know," Jeff said. "I'll get this batter out."

The next Red player up at bat hit the ball toward Ben again. Ben dove for the ball and came up with it.

"Good catch!" Jeff shouted out.

"Now we score some runs," Ben yelled back.

The first Tan player up struck out. Then Tim came up. He let one pitch go by for a ball. Then he got a hit. After that, one more Tan player was out, and Tim stole a base. There were two outs.

"I'm up," Jeff said. "Do you want someone to bat for me? We can use a big hit."

"No," Ben said, "you can hit as well as anyone. Just get up to the plate and concentrate. Watch for the pitch you can hit. Then slam it."

Jeff did what Ben said. He let one pitch go. It wasn't the pitch for him. Then he swung at a pitch. His hit shot up over first.

One of the Reds' outfielders ran after the ball. As Jeff got to first, he watched the ball vanish over the outfielder. He couldn't catch it. It was a home run! The game was over!

Jeff trotted around the bases, and his teammates clapped. Jeff's home run was the best hit of the game.

After Jeff stepped on home plate, he went over to Ben. "You were right, Ben," he said. "You helped me get that home run."

"No," Ben said, "it was your hit."

Jeff grinned. "Yes," Jeff said, "but you are special to all of us. You help us play like a team."

"That's right," Tim added. "You are something special, Ben, and a good friend, too."

Think About It

1. Why is Ben important to the team?

2. How does Ben help Jeff make a home run?

3. Jeff keeps a diary. What do you think he writes in his diary after the game in "Coach Ben"? Write his diary entry.

ROOM to SHARE

written by Julio Mendez

illustrated by Sandy Appleoff

Mike woke up and smiled. His grandpa was coming. That was the good news. Then Mom gave Mike the bad news.

"Make your room look good," Mom said. "Make room for Grandpa Ike, too. He'll be your roommate."

Mike sat right up. This was unexpected. Mike liked his grandpa, but he liked his room, too. It was all his. It was where he went when his baby sisters acted like pests.

"Mom," Mike griped. "My room is tiny. It's just the right size for me."

Mike's mom glanced over at Mike.

"In this family, we share," she said.

Mike longed for the comfort of a room for himself, but he said, "OK, Mom. I'll do it for the family."

"Thanks, Mike," Mom said. "That's fine."

She left for work, where she filled prescriptions.

When his grandpa came, Mike smiled
and hugged him. Inside, he was thinking
about sharing his room.

"I know I'll like being your roommate,"
Grandpa Ike said.

"Me, too," said Mike, but he could not
look at his grandpa.

"We'll have a good time," Grandpa
Ike went on. "Just the two of us."

At bedtime, Mike and his grandpa went to Mike's room. Mike's baby sisters wanted to come, too. They wanted attention from their grandpa.

"No," Grandpa Ike said, "not this time. This time it's just us men."

He winked at Mike, and Mike winked back. Grandpa Ike's good cheer was contagious. Maybe this would not be so bad after all.

In Mike's room, Grandpa Ike unpacked
his bags. He pulled out a wide blanket
and made a tent with it.

"Here we are in Camp Mike and Ike,"
he said.

Then he pulled out a tiny TV.

"We may be camping," he said,
"but we still like the comforts
of home."

Then Grandpa Ike got out a pile of snacks. He cut some pie for Mike.

"Now I'll tell you a family story," he said. "I'll tell you what your mom was like when she was nine. She was quite a bit like your baby sisters."

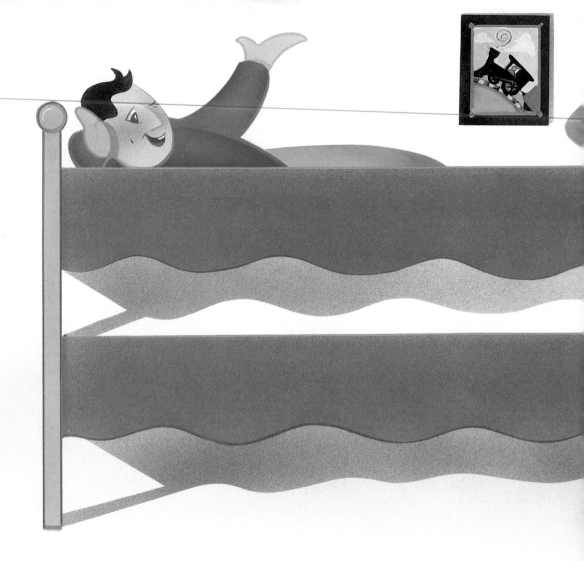

Mike had fun. He and his grandpa giggled and laughed. The time went by fast. Mike got very tired. He got into the top bunk to lie down.

Grandpa Ike said, "I like this, but it's too bad you have to share your room."

Mike smiled a wide smile.

"That's all right," he said. "There's room enough to share, and you are a fine roommate."

Think About It

1. How does Grandpa Ike make having a roommate fun for Mike?

2. When Mike says "Me, too" why can't he look at Grandpa?

3. After Grandpa Ike goes home, he will write Mike a thank-you note. Write the note he might send.

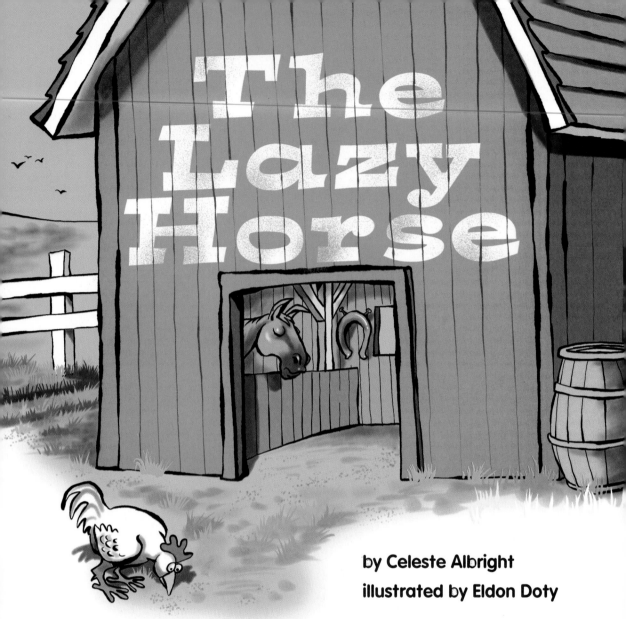

The Lazy Horse

by **Celeste Albright**

illustrated by **Eldon Doty**

A man had a horse and a dog. The faithful little dog lived in the house. She slept on the man's bed. Her food came from his plate.

The horse lived in the barn. He slept in a stall. He ate grass.

This horse wore no saddle. Nor did he do chores. He could roam without a care inside the gate. Yet the lazy horse did not recognize his good luck.

One morning before sunrise, the horse came up on the porch. A lamp illuminated the kitchen. The horse stared in.

The horse was amazed. He recognized the man and the dog inside. The dog chased her tail at a quick pace. Then she jumped up and sat next to the man. She ate food from his hand. The horse became aware that the man adored the dog. He looked at her with such pride!

The horse glared at them. With a shake of his mane, he stormed off the porch. That fortunate dog! Generations of horses had helped men persistently! Yet this man cared for dogs more.

The horse roamed the farm, careless of chicks and plants. His pride was hurt. As a horse, he had to live in the barn. He wanted to live in the house!

The horse knew what he must do. He must behave like the dog. So he trotted into the kitchen! But he was careless and bumbling—and so big! He made lots of mistakes.

He smashed the lamp. He broke the plates. The man turned pale and yelled, "Save me!"

The horse was ashamed, but the man forgave him. He summoned the horse and set him before a cart.

"A horse is a horse. You forgot that," he said. "But there is something you can do that a dog cannot."

No more was the horse lazy. He pulled the cart down the lane at a fast pace. What was the best part? Now the man was looking at *him* with pride!

What is the moral here?
Be content to be yourself.
Don't forget—you can do what some cannot!

Think About It

1. Why do you think the horse acted the way he did in the house?

2. Do you think the man really liked his dog more than his horse? Tell why you think as you do.

3. The dog and the chickens are talking about the horse and about what happened. Write what they say.

You Don't Mean It!

Do these sentences really mean what they say?

Shane put out the lights when he left the room.

Be sure to work out your math problems.

Wade read a tall tale.

Mr. Pate was fed up with his old car.

THE BRAVEST SOLDIER

by Glen Harlan   illustrated by Stephen Marchesi

My name is Tom Andrews. This is a story from my time as a soldier. I became a recruit when I was 17. My parents were sad to see me go. They could not persuade me to stay in my home town. I grew up in Blue Spring, but I wanted to move on.

I left one morning in June, when the grass was still wet with dew. With me was my best friend, Rube Jones. He played a happy tune on his flute as we left Blue Spring behind.

The training wasn't fun. The long hikes made me weary. I found it was important to listen to commands for clues. Then I did not become confused. When the training was over, I felt that I was a true soldier at last.

Rube did not think he was a true soldier. He did not like camping in the dark forest. He wanted to go back to Blue Spring.

Our colonel gave us a talk. He said, "It's normal for a soldier to be scared. The bravest soldiers I have commanded were scared at times."

His talk persuaded Rube to stay. I felt braver, too, now that Rube was staying.

After just a few weeks of training, the colonel said it was time for our first job. We would take fresh supplies to the next camp.

We would have to march for many days. To keep our spirits up along the way, some soldiers sang a marching song. Rube played the tune on his flute.

For three long days we marched. Even when
we felt weary, we had to go on. At last we
made it to the camp.

It was very quiet in the camp. We wondered
where all the soldiers were. We found them in
their tents, all very sick!

Then the colonel turned to Rube and me.
"Andrews and Jones," he said, "I need you to
take an urgent message. These men need a
doctor, quickly."

Rube was confused. "Why did the colonel pick us?" he asked.

"Rube, this is an urgent message," I said. "You and I are the fastest of the group. In fact, *you* are the fastest."

I persuaded Rube that we would do a fine job. We would stick together like glue. We would get a doctor for the men.

Rube and I ran through the forest and along the riverbank. We were almost back to our first camp and were very tired. Stumbling through the brambles that grew along the river, I fell and twisted my leg. Rube would have to go on alone. Just as he promised, he was back by dark. He had made it to camp and back in a flash! He had a doctor from the camp with him.

I met Rube with outstretched arms. He was a true friend. Now he was also a true soldier. He was the bravest soldier in the camp!

Think About It

1. What is Tom's life like in the army?

2. How do you think Tom feels when Rube goes on without him?

3. What do you think happens when Tom, Rube, and the doctor get back to the colonel? Write that part of the story.

Many Moons Ago

by Diane Hoyt-Goldsmith
illustrated by Franklin Ayers

Many moons ago, in the far north, it was dark all the time. This was because the sun, the moon, and the stars were hidden in three bags. The bags hung inside a mean man's house.

At that time, animals were very clever. They could sing and tell stories. Some could play tricks on those who were around.

Raven was one skillful creature. He could go as swiftly as an arrow over the land. Gazing down, he could see things happen from miles away.

Like all the rest of the animals, Raven was tired of the dark. He had a plan.

The mean man had a wife but no children. One time the wife was outside. Something made a tiny sound. "Gah! Gah!" it cried. She looked around and found a baby, all alone. She did not know the baby was Raven.

"Look," she said to the man. "I have found a baby who needs us." Then she made a big feast. She wanted to feed the baby. "Eat this," she said. "It's good for you."

Raven would not eat. All he would do was say "Gah! Gah! Gah!" He got louder and louder and louder.

The wife was sad. "What can we do?" she asked the man. "Our little baby will not eat."

"Maybe he wants a plaything," said the man. He looked at the three bags. He got down the bag with the stars and gave it to Raven. Raven stopped making his sounds and smiled.

Then Raven opened the bag. The stars tumbled out, and up they went. They arranged themselves into twinkling pictures of animals.

Raven smiled a little. Then he started to make his sounds again. "Gah! Gah! Gah!"

"Give him more things," said the wife. The man gave Raven the bag with the moon. When Raven opened the top, out came the moon. It rose over the canyon and lit up the dark. "Gah!" said Raven.

"No more playthings for you!" the man said.

When they were all in bed, Raven made more loud sounds. The wife was sad. The man tossed and turned. He could not sleep. "Gah! Gah! Gah!" Raven cried.

The man got down the last bag. He gave it to Raven. When Raven opened the bag, out came the sun, red and hot.

Up, up, up rose the sun. It lit up the deepest canyons and the darkest forests. All the animals could feel its heat.

Clever Raven shed his costume and showed what he was. "Gah!" he shouted with pride.

He still has not stopped. Even now you can hear him calling, "Gah! Gah! Gah!"

Think About It

1. How does Raven make the world different?

2. Why do you think Raven will not eat any of the feast the wife made?

3. How does the world look before Raven lets out the stars, the moon, and the sun? How does it look afterward? Draw two pictures. Write sentences to go with your pictures.

Your Answer, Please!

Q: Why is the moon always so sleepy?
  A: It stays up all night.

Q: Why did the fans want the sun's
  autograph?
  A: because it's such a big star

Q: How can you tell that the sun is happy?
  A: It's always beaming.

Q: Why don't astronauts feel crowded?
  A: They never run out of space.

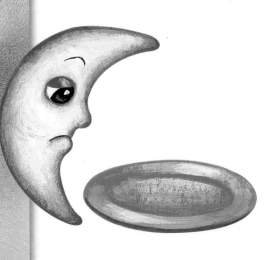

Q: How do you know that the
  moon is usually hungry?
  A: It is full only about once
    a month.

Q: Which day of the week is
  the stars' favorite?
  A: Sun-day.

Grandpa Tells Why

by Ann W. Phillips
illustrated by C.D. Hullinger

One year, the rains did not come to the plains. Day after day, the sun's rays burned down. The air was hot, and the ground was hard.

There was no hay. There was no grain. Many animals traveled very far away to look for things to eat.

The animals that stayed grumbled with hunger.

"We must have a council meeting," they said.

So a summons went out. Animals came from all over.

At the meeting, Gray Rabbit, Long-Tail Snake, and Grandpa Turtle were the wisest and bravest. They were the leaders.

"We can't stay here," the animals said. "We must find enough to eat."

So the animals set off over the plains staying close to their leaders. They hoped to find even the smallest tidbit to eat. They passed by many dangers during their hunt for a meal. Always Gray Rabbit, Long-Tail Snake, or Grandpa Turtle kept them safe.

At last they found a tree with good things to eat on it. The problem was the good things were way up on the branches. The animals could not reach them. They became alarmed.

"I know about this tree," said Grandpa Turtle. "We must say its name."

"Tell us why," the animals cried.

"It is a secret of the plains. The tree will let us eat when we repeat its name three times." said Grandpa Turtle.

"How can we find out the tree's name?" asked Gray Rabbit.

"The king knows it," said Grandpa Turtle. "It is his duty to tell it to us."

Gray Rabbit volunteered to go see the king.

The king had a fine mane of hair and a long tail. He looked angry to see Gray Rabbit.

Gray Rabbit was terrified, but she asked, "What is the tree's name?"

"Please-May-We," said the king. "Now go away."

On the way back Gray Rabbit fell in a hole. When she got out, she'd forgotten the tree's name.

"I will go this time," said Long-Tail Snake.

Long-Tail Snake traveled across the plains to see the king.

The king was very angry to be bothered again.

"What nonsense is this?" he growled.

Long-Tail Snake was terrified, but he asked, "What is the tree's name?"

"I will say it one more time," said the king. "The tree's name is Please-May-We. Now go away."

On the way back Long-Tail Snake fell in a hole. He was so shaken by the fall that he forgot the tree's name.

Now all the animals were afraid.
Who could get the name for them?

"I will go," said Grandpa Turtle. He started off over the plains.

The rest of the animals stayed by the tree and waited.

At last Turtle came to the king.

The king was very, very angry.

But Grandpa Turtle was not alarmed.

"What mischief is this?" roared the king.
"I told Gray Rabbit and Long-Tail Snake the name.
I will not tell YOU that the tree's name is Please-May-We."

"All right," said Grandpa Turtle.

He started back over the plains.

The animals waited and waited.

They were terrified that Grandpa Turtle would not make it back.

It took Grandpa Turtle many days, but he did not forget. Even when he fell in the hole he did not forget.

All the way across the plains he said the tree's name.

At last he came to the tree.

"What is the tree's name?" the animals asked.

"Please-May-We," said Grandpa Turtle.

The animals repeated the name three times, then the tree bent down.

It laid good things to eat on the ground.

The animals ate and ate until they were satisfied.

From then on, Grandpa Turtle was the first one the animals asked when they wondered why something was the way it was.

Think About It

1. Why can't Gray Rabbit and Long-Tail Snake get things to eat from the tree? How does Grandpa Turtle get the tree to help the animals?

2. Why do you think Gray Rabbit and Long-Tail Snake are terrified of the king?

3. Rabbit, Snake, and Turtle each try to solve the problem of the tree. Make a chart to show how these characters are alike, and how they are different.

The Snow Baby

by Robert Newell

illustrated by Cheryl Kirk Noll

Just below a mountain lived a farmer and his wife. Their crops were green. Their goats were fat. Still, sorrow hung over the farm like a dark shadow. You see, these two wanted a baby of their own. Without that, life seemed hollow.

Late one evening, a full moon hung low over the mountain. The farmer watched his wife gazing out the window. A tear ran down her tender cheek.

It made the farmer furious to see his gentle wife so sad. Yet he pretended to smile, for her sake.

"Dear Willow!" he said. "What do you see out that window?"

"I see a baby," his wife said with a sob. "She's on the top of the mountain."

"Willow, you know that can't be. That's the glow from the moon on the snow."

"Perhaps," Willow said. Slow tears ran down her cheeks. The farmer knew what he must do.

"I am going to the mountain," he said to his wife. "If there's a baby there, I must save it."

"But that's a terrible journey!" Willow cried.

The farmer did not want Willow to fear for him. "I work hard. I have the strength of two men. I will not fail you." He embraced Willow and lifted the latch. "Expect me tomorrow at dusk," he said.

Indeed, it was a terrible journey. A furious wind was blowing. Snow began to fall. The road ended, and the farmer had to pull himself up narrow cliffs. The brittle, frozen snow groaned and moaned. At any time, it could fall in.

The farmer's strength was giving out, but he kept going. He could not fail his wife.

When the farmer got home, he held a tiny bundle in his cloak. He showed his wife a baby girl. Willow was delighted. "Come to me, my little pea pod," she said. The glowing moon seemed to smile on the family.

At last the farmer and his wife had a baby of their own. What a dear little girl she was! They called her Snowflake, for she was found in the snow. Willow brushed her soft hair and kissed her tender little toes.

Now the farm was aglow with happiness. Snowflake was the best of girls. She played and worked and grew. In the wink of an eye, she was all grown up.

Hopeful fellows began to show up at the farm to see Snowflake. Some were handsome. Some were rich. Each wanted Snowflake to be his wife.

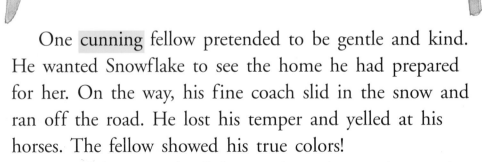

One cunning fellow pretended to be gentle and kind. He wanted Snowflake to see the home he had prepared for her. On the way, his fine coach slid in the snow and ran off the road. He lost his temper and yelled at his horses. The fellow showed his true colors!

Snowflake got out of the coach, and turned toward home. Her parents had saved her from a snowy mountain. Now, the snow showed her the way home to her parents!

Think About It

1. Is "The Snow Baby" a good title for this story? Tell why or why not.

2. Do you think the farmer was wise to go to the mountain to look for a baby? Explain.

3. A kind and gentle young man comes to visit Snowflake. Write what happens next.

ADVICE

eauregard

Mr. Gold

Jo

Ms. Post

Speaker

Time: A Friday morning in the middle of summer.

Stage setting: The Gold home; we can see the yard outside as well as the inside of the house.

Mrs. Gold: Peter! Jo! Brian! Please don't leave your things in the middle of the room where I can keep falling over them!

Peter: But Mom, where can we put them?

Jo: There's no room anywhere.

Brian: Our house is so tiny! We're bumping elbows each time we turn around.

Mrs. Gold: I know, but there's no way to fix this problem.

Peter: Father, can you find us a bigger house?

Mr. Gold: No, we can't afford a bigger house. I'll speak with Ms. Post, because she is the wisest person in town. She may have some ideas or some good advice.

159

Speaker: One morning, Ms. Post came over to the Gold home.

Mr. Gold: *(looking sad)* Hi, Ms. Post. Thank you for stopping by. My family has a big problem.

Ms. Post: What kind of problem?

Mr. Gold: Our house is so tiny that we have no room. We have a dreadful time moving about. What can we do?

Ms. Post: I see you have hens in your yard. Bring them into the house with you.

Mr. Gold: But Ms. Post, I'm confused. How will that help?

Ms. Post: Just do as I say and you'll see. Good day. *(She leaves.)*

Speaker: Mr. Gold let the hens into the house.

Peter: Father! What are you doing?

Jo: We can't have hens in our tiny house!

Brian: *(wailing)* I just stepped on an egg and now it's broken!

Mrs. Gold: There are feathers all over! Get those hens out of here!

Mr. Gold: We must follow Ms. Post's advice. She said to bring them in, and we will keep them in until I can speak with her again. After all, she is the wisest person in town.

Mrs. Gold: Please ask her to return. Tell her we have no room!

Speaker: Ms. Post returned to the Gold home.

Mr. Gold: Ms. Post, look at the kind of mess we're in now!

Ms. Post: I see you have goats and cows in your yard. Bring them into the house with you, too.

Mrs. Gold: Oh! Please, no! We have less room than before!

Ms. Post: Just do as I say, and you'll see. Good day. *(She leaves.)*

Mr. Gold: This will be dreadful, but we'll do as she says! After all, Ms. Post is the wisest person in town.

Speaker: Mr. Gold let the goats and both cows come in.

Peter: Father, hold on a moment! How can you do this?

Jo: We have no room for goats and cows in here!

Brian: I'm sitting on a goat!

Mr. Gold: We must trust Ms. Post. She told me to bring them in, and we all know that she is the wisest person in town.

Mrs. Gold: Please ask her to return. Tell her we have no room!

Speaker: Ms. Post returned to the Gold home.

Ms. Post: How are you faring now, Mr. Gold?

Mr. Gold: We're going out of our minds! We've lost our wits! We have no room for all these animals!

Ms. Post: *(smiling)* Then take them outside again. Farewell, Mr. Gold. *(She leaves. He takes all the animals back into the yard.)*

Peter: Father! Our house seems so much bigger now!

Mrs. Gold: We have so much more room!

Mr. Gold: I told you! Ms. Post gives good advice.

Think About It

1. What problem did the Golds have? What advice did Ms. Post give them?

2. Do you think Ms. Post gives the Golds good advice? Tell why you think as you do.

3. Think of some good advice a wise person has given you. Write a short story for a younger child that shows why this advice is good to follow.

Auction Day

by Carol Storment

illustrated by Anthony Carnabuci

When Ty spied the pony in the pen of wild horses, he knew what he had to do. First he went to the bank.

"How much money do I have?" he asked.

The man smiled. "You're a rich man, Tyrone. You have six dollars."

"Is that enough for that pony outside?" asked Ty.

The man looked out the window. "Oh no, Ty. Those horses will go for ten dollars or more. Besides, what good would a wild pony be on a farm?"

Ty didn't say another word. He went across the road to the store. Ty had a plan to get his pony.

"Is there any work I could do for you, Mrs. Wyman?" Ty asked. "I need some extra money."

The storekeeper said, "Why yes, Tyrone. I'll find something for you to do."

Ty started by sweeping up. All morning he worked around the store, stacking shelves and cleaning the back room. When he was done, Mrs. Wyman gave him a dollar.

Ty walked by the pen full of wild horses. There she was, the littlest pony. Her coat was so black, it was almost blue. "Hello, Blue Sky," Ty said. He put out his hand. The shy pony jumped away. Her eyes were wild, but they looked sad, too.

"Be brave, girl!" Ty said. "You'll be out of here tomorrow."

The next day, Ty went to see three of his neighbors. He asked each one, "Is there work I can do for you?"

"You bet there is!" they all said.

First, Ty cut tall grass for Mr. Dyer. Then he moved a pile of rocks for Mr. Ryan. He fed chickens and collected eggs for Mrs. Bly. He worked until Mrs. Bly fried some eggs for his lunch. She asked Ty what he needed the money for.

"A pony" was all he would say. Then he went back to work. Ty tried his best to do each task well. He wanted his neighbors to be satisfied with his work.

When Ty was done, each neighbor was happy and paid him one dollar. Now he had three more dollars! The neighbors watched as he left for home. "That Tyrone works hard," they all agreed. "But he'll have his hands full if he tries to tame a wild pony!"

When Ty got home, he got out his bank. He counted all his money. Then he borrowed a horse and rode as fast as he could into town. He ran to the bank. It was still open.

"I'll take my six dollars, please," Ty told the man.

The man smiled. "Here you go. Good luck at the sale tomorrow!"

The sale started early. Everyone in the county came to see the wild horses. Ty was there with his money clutched in his hand.

The auctioneer called out that it was time to start. The bids began. The horses were going for much more than ten dollars. Ty felt like crying. He wouldn't have enough money!

At last only Blue Sky was left. Ty bid ten dollars. Everyone in town knew how much Ty wanted that pony. No one said a word.

"Sold!" shouted the auctioneer. "That pony is all yours, son."

All of Ty's neighbors clapped for him.

Ty and his family got Blue Sky home and into her new pen. Ty sat and watched her for a while. Her blue-black coat was glistening in the sun. Her mane was flying in the wind. But her eyes were still wild and sad. Then Ty got up and opened the gate. Blue Sky shot out and galloped away.

His father ran up. "Ty! Why did you let the pony get away? You worked so hard to get the money for her!"

Ty said, "Blue Sky would never be happy living on a farm. I was glad to spend my money to set her free."

Ty felt proud as his pony galloped to freedom. *Fly away, Blue Sky!*

Think About It

1. What does Ty do so that he can buy Blue Sky?

2. Why do you think Ty doesn't tell anyone he plans to set Blue Sky free?

3. Write the diary entry Ty might write the day he lets Blue Sky go.

Just Horsing Around

As I was swimming after school,
A pony jumped into the pool,
And this is what he said:
"That's one hot sun up in the sky.
My hooves were just about to fry!
I'll cool them off instead."

"Neigh! With four feet instead of two,
This swimming stuff is hard to do—
But it won't hurt to try!"
That pony splished and splashed around
And sloshed the water on the ground
Until the pool was dry!

A Cookie for the Cowboys

by Caren B. Stelson
illustrated by Jerry Tiritilli

Howdy, partner! Glad to have you riding along on this cattle drive. My name's George Gemson, but you can call me Cookie. Everyone does. My job is to cook for all you cowhands out on the range. You stay on the good side of me and you won't go hungry.

You look like a greenhorn to me. You know what that means? You're a brand-new hand. I'm sure the trail boss is a fair judge of skill, so you must be good with horses. I've been on more than my share of cattle drives. I'll tell you what's in store for you.

Tending cattle is hard work. You'll be riding a horse all day long. You'll be very dirty. You'll eat dust. We'll move the cattle north slowly, so they have time to eat and grow fat. Keep an eye out for stray cows. These ranchers want their cattle herds to bring a good price in the market. They want to make money—a profit. That's OK by me. Then we'll all be paid.

The day starts early on a cattle drive. You'll be up at sunrise. I'll be up before that. I start breakfast at three in the morning. First, I make up a roaring campfire. Next, I bake the rolls. Then I make the coffee. Last, I put the beans in the pot and fry up the bacon. All this takes time. I won't nudge you gently to wake you up. When I holler that breakfast is ready, you'd better come running.

This is my wagon. It's called a chuck wagon. Mr. Charles Goodnight made the first one in 1866. He got an old army wagon and nailed a dresser to the back of it. Folks called Mr. Goodnight "Chuck." Maybe that's how this wagon got its name. Greenhorn, this wagon will be your home away from home.

I'll show you what I mean. I keep everything in
this dresser. I keep all the dry stuff in this one.
Here's the flour, beans, coffee—and the honey, too.
Here is where I keep the tin plates, cups, and forks.
This one is for the trail boss. He keeps his papers
and maps safe in my chuck wagon.

This next one holds stuff for any doctoring I might have to do on the trail. If a snake bites you, let me know. If you want a haircut, you let me know about that, too. I'm a jack-of-all-trades.

Well, partner, I can't talk all day. You go on over to the corral. Pick out a gentle horse that's been well tamed. Then be ready for the time of your life. Yippee!

Think About It

1. Is Cookie's job easy? What kinds of things does he do?

2. Why does Cookie start cooking breakfast at three in the morning?

3. Cookie is important to the cowboys. Write a poem or words to a song that the cowboys might write about their cook.

How Grandmama

Tamed the West

by Celeste Albright
illustrated by John Manders

This is my grandmother, Mrs. Emma Lee Main, of High Mount, Tennessee. Wasn't she a fine little miss? You bet she was—and downright clever, too!

My grandmother liked to bake delicious cakes and delightful fruit pies. But Grandmama liked excitement, too. We children had wild rides in her wagon. She entertained us with frightful tales each night by candlelight. We all adored her.

In time, however, Grandmama found life in High Mount too tame. She craved more excitement. So Grandmama went out West. She started a stagecoach business.

My stars! How she did make those horses run! Why, once they left Mud Flats on a Saturday. They had to go to Dry Gulch, fifteen miles away. They ran so fast, they got there by nightfall on Friday— the day before they started! Grandmama entertained the travelers by singing as she drove.

Grandmama busted broncos, too. She didn't have to fight them. She just baked one of her delicious apple pies in a skillet. Those wild horses sat right up and begged like dogs!

After a little while, Grandmama got bored driving that stagecoach. She needed some new excitement.

Overnight, Mrs. Emma Lee Main became a miner. She got a mule named Fred and loaded him up with picks, pans, and shovels. All that gear was not light, and Fred was a sorrowful sight. Grandmama noticed his plight and just picked him up! Then off they went to dig for gold.

I wish I had a nickel
for every shovelful of dirt
Grandmama dug. I'd be rich
by now! She dug in daylight,
twilight, and moonlight. When
there was no moon, she dug by
starlight. Nothing could stop her.
The pile of dirt got so high, it
became a landmark in the town
of Pike. People called it Pike's
Peak. It was such a sight that
people came from miles around.
Many of them settled there, and
Pike became a boom town.

Luck was with Grandmama. She found two big nuggets the very first day. One golden lump was the size of her fist. The other was as big as a skillet!

My, my, how the miners did sigh and weep! They had been digging for years and might never make a strike.

Grandmama had all the gold she and Fred could tote. The mining business was getting boring to her anyway. So Grandmama set her gear on a shelf and moved on.

After Grandmama left the mining business, she became a sheriff. Land sakes, what a fright she gave those wild cowhands! She made them take notice, all right.

When bank robbers saw Grandmama coming, they were downright scared. They ran like lightning to the jail and locked themselves in!

Grandmama never did settle in one spot. Once a town was tamed, all the excitement was over. Things got quiet, and quiet was too boring for her.

Grandmama moved from boom town to boom town. She broke up the fights, filled up the jails, and moved on.

The towns were very grateful to Grandmama. They wanted to thank her, and they found just the right way.

Do you know why so many towns have a street called Main Street? Think about it.

Those streets are named after Mrs. Emma Lee Main—my wild-west-taming grandmama!

Think About It

1. What kinds of work did Grandmama do out West?

2. How do you know that the person telling the story is proud of Grandmama?

3. Grandmama sent a postcard to a friend. She told about one of her adventures. Write the postcard she sent.

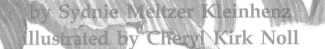

HARVEST TIME

by Sydnie Meltzer Kleinhenz
illustrated by Cheryl Kirk Noll

"It's harvest time, Lizzie," Dad said.

Mom said, "How about a harvest party tomorrow?"

I clapped my hands. Dad nodded. "Everybody bring a memory-maker," he called as he hurried off to work.

We don't always get a harvest from our banana trees. Bananas grow well in the tropics, but we live on Galveston Island. Sometimes the Texas winter is too cold for banana plants. Sometimes a tropical storm blows off the flowers. Then no fruit can grow. The years we do get bananas, we have a harvest party.

On Saturday morning I went to the trading market. I was looking for a memory-maker. At last I found the perfect thing—a tiny plastic sailing schooner. It was a bargain, so I got it and ran home.

First, I glued the little ship on the inside of a jar lid. Next, I put glitter and water in the jar. Last, I put on the lid and taped around it. I finished the memory-maker just as Dad called, "Harvest time, party time!"

We all met on a blanket on the grass. When I looked up, it seemed as if the banana leaves reached as high as the sky. Some of the bananas were still green. Some were as yellow as the bus I ride each day.

Dad put my spelling folder on the blanket. "Here is my memory-maker," he said. "I'm thankful to my Grandma and Grandpa Jakoby. When they came to America, they studied hard to speak English. That helped them find good jobs and get this fine house."

Mom's memory-maker was a mixing bowl. "I'm thankful that Grandma and Grandpa Jakoby planted bananas. Now we can eat them as snacks or bake tasty treats with them."

I turned my memory-maker upside down and gave it a shake. The glitter looked like swirly snow around the ship.

"I'm thankful that Dad's Grandma and Grandpa Jakoby left their cold and snowy home. I'm glad the ship sailed safely to Galveston Island. I like living where it's mostly warm and sunny."

Mom gave me a squeeze. "You're not the only one who likes it sunny," she said.

Dad told the rest of our family story. Then he got his machete and said, "Let's cut bananas."

Mom and I helped support the bunch as Dad cut the stem. It felt as if we were holding a big log up in the air! My arms were rubbery when we softly set the bananas on the blanket.

We packed small bunches of bananas in bags and carried them to our neighbors. Then it was party time!

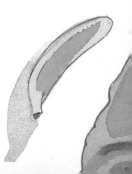

First we broke bananas into the blender. Mom added milk, Dad added sweetener, and I added ice. Dad hit the button to whir the mix into milkshakes. The river of banana foam felt frosty all the way down to my belly! We put the extra drink mix into molds to freeze solid. We would have banana ice pops for later.

After that, we mashed bananas to a pulp. We made pans and pans of banana muffins. Some were to give away. Some were to freeze and save. We nibbled banana muffins as we cleaned up.

I filled up on plenty of banana treats. And we all made plenty of memories to last until next harvest time.

Think About It

1. Why does the family bring memory-makers to the harvest party?

2. How often do Lizzie and her mom and dad have a harvest party? How do you know?

3. The next time they get bananas, Lizzie invites other family members to the harvest party. Make the invitation she sends. Use words and pictures in the invitation.

On the Farm

Q: What did the farmer say when he was sick?

> **A:** I don't field so good.

Q: Do you know how long cows should be milked?

> **A:** the same way as short cows

Q: Do you believe that carrots are good for your eyes?

> **A:** Yes, because not many rabbits wear glasses.

Q: Why do cows wear bells?

> **A:** because their horns don't work

Q: What is the chief part of a horse?

> **A:** the mane part

Q: Why did the farmer drive a steamroller over his field?

> **A:** He wanted to raise mashed potatoes.

197

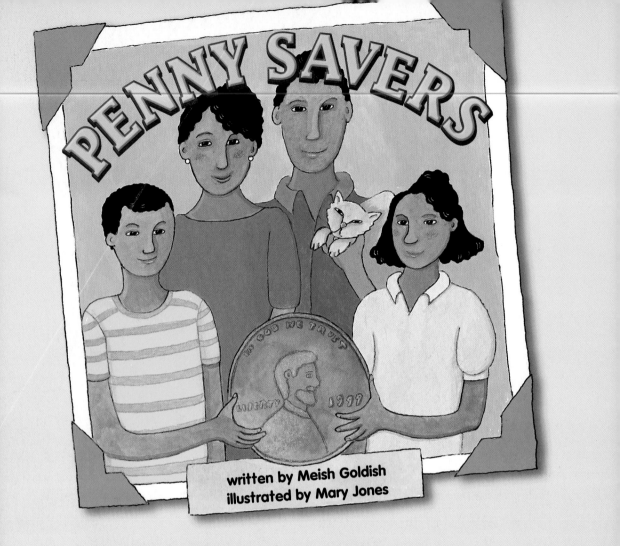

PENNY SAVERS

written by Meish Goldish
illustrated by Mary Jones

"A penny saved is a penny earned."

Did you ever hear that saying? It means that if you can hold on to money and not spend it, you have really earned it.

Why save your money? What's the point? Why not spend it right away and enjoy it now?

The Boyd family knows why. Let's see what they have found out.

Roy Boyd will turn nine years old on his birthday this month. Each year, Roy receives money for his birthday. He likes to spend it right away. He spends each dollar and doesn't save a thing.

Last year, Roy went to the toy store the day after his birthday. He got a yo-yo and a ball. The next week he found a toy car he wanted. He couldn't buy it because he had no more money.

This year, Roy will save his birthday money until he knows all his choices. Then he'll buy what he wants most.

Roy has found out why it's smart to save.

Joy Boyd is Roy's sister. Like Roy, Joy gets money each year for her birthday. Like Roy, she likes to spend each dollar right away.

This year Joy wanted to get skates, but she did not receive enough money to buy them.

At first, Joy said to herself, "The skates cost too much. I guess I'll have to buy something that costs less."

Then Joy had an idea. "I'll save all my birthday money this year," she said. "Maybe I can work to earn the rest of the money I'll need to buy the skates."

Joy has discovered how it helps to save.

Mrs. Boyd knows that a penny saved is a penny earned. In fact, she saves more than just pennies. She saves all kinds of coins.

Sometimes Mrs. Boyd rides the bus to work. The driver does not take dollar bills, so the riders must pay with combinations of coins. If they don't have the right amount of coins, they can't ride.

All week, Mrs. Boyd makes it a point to save her coins. She uses dollar bills to pay for things and saves her change. That way, she'll have coins when she wants to ride the bus.

Like his wife, Mr. Boyd spends his money carefully. He knows the value of a dollar and that it pays to save.

Mr. Boyd puts the money he earns in a bank. Why? First of all, he knows the money is safe there and that it won't get lost. Mr. Boyd and his wife go to the bank and take out cash when they need it. They can also pay for things by writing checks. Then the bank sends the money to the person who received the check.

When the Boyds save money in a bank, they make money, too! That's because the bank pays them to save their money there. If you save your money in a bank, you'll make money, too!

It really does "pay" to save!

The Boyds have found out something else about saving money. You never know when you'll need it!

Last year, it rained very hard on the Boyds' home. The roof began to leak and needed to be fixed right away.

The Boyds hired someone to fix their roof. It cost a lot of money. What if they had not saved? They could not have had the work done, and the rain would have left their home soiled and spoiled.

You never know when you may need money. That's why it's wise to "save for a rainy day."

Now you know why the Boyds save their money. They know that it is important to make choices about spending and saving. You may wish to save, too. How can you get started?

You may receive some money as a gift on your birthday. Maybe you can earn an allowance for doing chores around the house. You might make the beds, sweep the floor, and take out the trash. You could also offer to clean the yard for your neighbors.

You may think of a hundred ways to make money! A hundred jobs may get you a hundred dollars or more. If you can save it, congratulations!

Think About It

1. What reasons does the author give for saving money?

2. What does "saving for a rainy day" mean?

3. The Boyd family is having a meeting. They are talking about what to do with $50 that Grandma sent them. Write what each person might say.

BOOK OF DAYS

written by
Deborah Akers

illustrated by
Mercedes McDonald

Date: April 2

Dear Sue,

I felt so blue after you drove away! Now I have a plan. I will keep each day in this book until my big sister is home again. Then you can read about everything you missed, and I will feel less lonely.

I put myself in charge of your flower box. There were three new green sprouts in the soil. You said there would soon be a rainbow of flowers. I poured a little more water to hurry them along. I could tell they wondered where you were.

Date: April 6

Dear Sue,

Today was a good day. We worked in the garden, and Mom put me in charge of the carrot seeds. I pushed them into the dirt the way you showed me.

Remember last fall, when we dug beds for the plants to sleep in? Most of them are still sleeping, but a few seem to be stirring. The sweet pea sprouts are reaching for the sun with soft, curly fingers.

Date: April 9

Dear Sue,

Today I put myself in charge of the fruit trees. I walked down every row, admiring the blossoms. I counted all the trees that have buds.

Here is a branch from the apple tree. Remember when we picked a basketful of apples? Then you helped me bake my first pie. I felt like a real cook!

The trees seem as if they are holding secrets in their tight buds. I think they are waiting for the right person to share them with. I know just how they feel.

Date: April 13

Dear Sue,

Today was an average day. While Mom went into town, Dad and I walked down to the river. I collected rocks for you on the beach. There were lots of beautiful ones, but I was choosy. I took just a few you could put on your desk.

Guess what happened next? I saw tracks in the sand! Our friend the fox is back, with some baby foxes, too. That must mean spring is really here. When will you be home? You're missing everything!

Date: April 21

Dear Sue,

Today the sky could not stop crying, and your flower box was swimming in rain. I watched from the porch as pools grew in the garden. The fruit trees shook in the storm.

A good thing happened today, too—there was a rainbow. I remembered the special rainbow wish we always make when it rains. I made my wish. Mom said she had a feeling it would come true soon.

Date: April 22

Dear Sue,

Mom was right! I woke up to a sunny day and ran outside. I think the garden must have heard a signal in the night. There were leaves and blooms and little celebrations everywhere!

Then came the best news! You are coming home tonight! Now I am putting myself in charge of the biggest celebration of all!

Welcome Home, Sue

Think About It

1. Why does the girl write in her book of days? What does she write about?

2. Do you think the girl in the story will go on writing in her book of days? Tell why you think as you do.

3. Imagine that a friend or family member is out of town. Write a journal entry for a special day you would want him or her to know about.

Summer's Too Short

"Summer's too short," said the kangaroo.
"I've books to read. I've things to do.
I'll celebrate, with a happy shout,
How glad I am that school is out.

"I'll start by cooking up some noodles.
They're my favorites—I'll eat oodles!
I'll swim some laps around the pool
To keep my furry body cool.

"I'll play with buddies, watch TV,
Read every book in the library.
I'll sit and dream and nap some, too.
Hmmm. There's nothing left to do.

"Summertime is getting boring.
The days are long—I'm almost snoring.
I must confess that in my heart,
I just can't wait for school to start!"

213

THE HUMMINGBIRD
• GARDEN •

Cyrus already knew what Dad would say. He had to ask anyway.

"Dad, may we get a pet? Please! We really need a pet around here."

"You know we can't have a pet," Dad said. "The rule is no dogs in this building. Hamsters make you sneeze, and the city is no place for a pony!"

WRITTEN BY JOSÉ GONZALES
ILLUSTRATED BY JOUNG UN KIM

Cy smiled at Dad's little joke, but he still felt bad.

Then Dad said, "I have an idea. City birds need help. You can use the backyard to make a garden for them. The birds can be your pets."

"Oh, Dad," Cy said. "Our backyard is made of cement! There's no space for a garden out there!" He knew Dad was doing his best, but he didn't understand how that idea could work.

"You can make space," Dad said. "You can use things our neighbors throw out to plant flowers in. You can dig up dirt to put in them. I'll give you a few dollars to get seeds and a bird feeder."

"I'll try it," said Cy. Maybe Dad's idea was not so bad after all.

That same evening, Cy looked through bird books.

"I want our bird visitors to be hummingbirds," Cy told Dad.

"Good idea," Dad replied. "Our little garden has ample space for such tiny birds."

"Hummingbirds catch and eat bugs," Cy went on. "They drink the nectar from flowers. Sometimes they drink sweet water from a feeder, too. They like red and pink flowers best, so I'll plant red and pink flowers to attract them to the garden. Once they're here, they'll find the feeder. Then they'll know where to visit when they're thirsty."

Cy looked through the neighbors' junk. He picked up old boxes and pails, then he poked holes in the bottoms so the water would drain out. When Mrs. Cecil found out what he was doing, she gave him old pots from her cellar. Cy filled everything with dirt.

Soon Cy was ready to get his seeds. Dad gave him some money and took him to the shopping center.

Back at home, Cy dug little furrows in the dirt and planted seeds for red flowers. He watered the seeds each day and watched for signs of growth.

When Cy spied red flowers in his garden, he mixed up some sweet water. He filled the hummingbird feeder. Then he waited for thirsty hummingbirds.

Cy watched from morning to evening. No little visitors showed up. It seemed that the hummingbirds had shunned his beautiful garden.

Then one summer day Cy spotted a tiny blur. Could it be? Yes! It was a hummingbird. It raced around the garden like a small cyclone. Its wings were going like little windmills. It found the feeder, and soon more hummingbirds joined it.

Each day, Cy's visitors returned. They circled the flowers and sucked sweet water from the feeder. Cy could see their red throats. He looked in his bird book and found that they were ruby-throated hummingbirds.

In the evenings, Cy took down the feeder. He cleaned it out and filled it with fresh sweet water. Then he put it up again. He knew the daytime heat would bring his visitors back.

Cy liked to watch the tiny birds. Their wings went so fast that they were just a blur. They could hang in one place like a helicopter! Cy cherished the time he spent with his new pets.

The days got shorter, and there was less heat. Summer turned to fall. One day the hummingbirds did not return. Cy missed his little pets, but he knew they had to go south. They could not stand winter's snow and ice.

He cleaned the feeder one last time and put it away. He knew he would need it again. Next spring he would plant a new garden. He would put up the feeder, and his pets would visit again. Cy had turned his cement backyard into a very nice place for hummingbirds.

Think About It

1. What does Cy do to make a garden for his pets? How long do his pets stay?

2. How do you think Cy's dad feels about the changes Cy makes in the garden? Tell why you think as you do.

3. A newspaper reporter came and looked at Cy's hummingbird garden. She took pictures and wrote a news story about what Cy had done. Write the newspaper story, and draw a picture to go with it.

A MOUNTAIN
BLOWS ITS TOP

A chain of mountains runs along the west coast of North America. It's called the Cascade Range.

The mountains in this range are beautiful. Visitors hike and camp there. Loggers cut trees for lumber. Birds and animals make their homes in the forests, fields, and rivers.

STORY BY KANA RILEY

These peaks were formed long ago by volcanoes. Deep in the center of our planet is hot melted rock called magma. On top of it float plates of hard rock that form the planet's crust.

In 1980 the plates under the Cascade Range started to shift. The edges of the plates pushed up magma. As the magma rose, it caused the north side of Mount St. Helens to bulge. It made the ground shake. Plumes of steam began to shoot out of the old crater, or hole, at the top. Was the mountain ready to blow? No one knew.

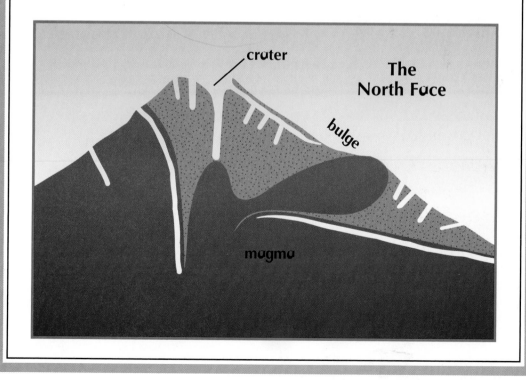

crater

The North Face

bulge

magma

Sunday, May 18, 1980, dawned clear. Snowcapped Mount St. Helens caught the early rays of the sun. All seemed peaceful.

Then suddenly, at 8:32 A.M., the ground began to shake. The epicenter of this quake was very near Mount St. Helens.

This was a big one! With a mighty blast, it cracked the side of the mountain. Magma gushed to the surface, pushing layers of dirt and rocks and water in front of it. Blast after blast rocked the mountain.

Blocks of ice went flying. Water turned to steam. Rocks exploded into dust. Hot ash flew 12 miles into the sky.

Yakima, Washington, is 85 miles from Mount St. Helens. By 9:30 A.M. the sky in Yakima began to grow black. Lightning flashed. It looked as if a storm were coming.

But it was not rain that fell. It was ash. The tiny bits had edges as sharp as glass. They hurt everyone's eyes and made it hard to breathe.

All day ash fell. Soon every surface was covered with layers of it. Workers later swept up more than 600,000 tons from the streets and buildings.

When the big blasts stopped, Mount St. Helens was an awesome sight. The top of the mountain was not there. In its place was a huge, gray hole. From the center of it, clouds of ash still puffed into the air.

The land around the mountain looked like the surface of the moon. All was still. Trees were spilled all over the ground like match sticks. Rivers were choked with mud. Most of the animals had been caught by the blasts. No birds sang.

It has been many years since the mountain blew. What has Mount St. Helens taught us?

It has taught us that our planet is always changing. The blast showed us the awesome damage these changes can cause.

Yet we also saw that in time the land will heal. New plants now grow out of the layers of ash. Animals have come back. The rivers run clear once more.

What's going on inside the mountain? It's not quiet yet. In the center of the crater, another dome of magma is growing. Sometimes steam and ash gush out of it. They help us remember that our planet is still alive and still shaking.

Think About It

1. What happened when Mount St. Helens erupted? What has happened since then?

2. Will Mount St. Helens erupt again? What makes you think as you do?

3. Think about life in Yakima on the day Mount St. Helens blew its top. Write a diary entry as if you were there that day.

Tongue Tanglers

Challenge your tongue! Give it a workout by saying the names of these mountains.

Begin with **Kilimanjaro.**

Say kil•uh•muhn•JAR•oh. This snowy peak, which adventurers often try to climb, is in the African country of Tanzania.

Now try **Chimborazo.**

Say chim•buh•RAH•zoh. This volcano rises in Ecuador, in South America.

Can you say **Popocatepetl?**

Say poh•puh•kat•uh•PET•uhl. This volcano stands close to Mexico City.

Are you ready for **Llullaillaco?**

Say yoo•y-eye•YAHK•oh. This volcano is on the border between Argentina and Chile in South America.

Now you can show off to your friends by saying **Kilimanjaro, Chimborazo, Popocatepetl, Llullaillaco.**

Doesn't that just flow off your tongue?

THE PLACE IN SPACE

Written by Susan M. Fischer
Illustrated by Paul Meisel

Mom came into my room and sat on the edge of my bed. "Good night, Will," she said, wrapping her cool hand around my wrist. "Where are you off to tonight?" she asked. "Grandma's garden? The lake? The moon?" Mom knew that my dreams could take me places.

"I just might go far out into the universe, Mom," I said. "I bet I could explore the entire world in a single night!"

She smiled and said, "I bet you could, too, dear. Sweet dreams." She pulled the blanket she knitted for me right up to my chin. "We can converse about it in the morning," she said with a wink.

"Sure, Mom." I yawned as she turned on my night-light. It's a blue-and-green sphere that glows as it twirls. I watched it for a while. Eventually I fell asleep.

At first I wondered where I was, but then I knew.
I was on top of my very own mountain. I'd been
here a thousand times before, but it had never looked
as beautiful as this. I could see the entire city where
I live. I found the winding river and the town hall.

Up above me, a bird was circling—my friend the
wren. She was calling to me. "Yes! Here I come!" I
replied. I soared up and followed her. Up and away
we flew, higher and higher!

As we sailed over misty, puffy clouds, I looked
down and saw my entire state, its shape outlined by
a river. It looked just like the map in my classroom.
It got littler and littler as we flew higher and higher.

Soon I could see our country between two big
seas. Our country is as wide as the whole continent!
Up and up and up we flew, as if we were never
going to stop.

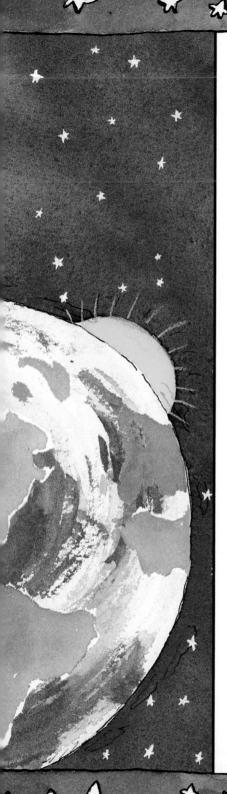

Then I couldn't believe my eyes. I had to blink several times. Could it be the world? I saw our beautiful planet as a huge, green-and-blue sphere. There were clouds and light and darkness all around it. It was even prettier than my night-light.

The wren and I watched the world turn, happy to be together and to share this sight. Then the sun began to peek around. I knew it was almost morning, and eventually we would have to begin our long flight homeward.

There was a little knock at my door. Mom said, "It's time to rise and shine. How was your night?"

"Oh, Mom, it was wonderful," I said. "I wish you could have been there."

My night-light was still glowing as it twirled. Just then we could hear a bird singing. I smiled because I knew it was my friend the wren.

Think About It

1. Where does Will go in his dream? Who goes with him?

2. How do you think Will's mom knows that he travels in his dreams?

3. What would you see if you looked down on your town from up in the sky? Draw a picture showing how things would look. Label the parts of your picture.

A METEOR Stopped Here

by Kana Riley
illustration by Mel Grant

Our planet gets many kinds of visitors from space. Comets are one kind.

A comet is a ball of frozen gases. The gases are the nucleus, or center, of the comet.

Around the nucleus is a cloud. The cloud looks like a tail. That's because a force from the sun called solar wind blows the cloud out behind the comet.

At night a comet glows like a fluorescent light. It reflects light from the sun, and we see that reflected glow.

Comets loop around the sun in orbits. We know some of their orbits well enough to tell when they will pass near us.

Billions of meteors are also part of our solar system. They orbit the sun, too.

Meteors are different from comets. They are solid, like rock, and most of them show up without warning.

Every day, millions of little meteors enter our atmosphere, the air around our planet. Most are tiny particles. They are about the size of a grain of sand.

When these little meteors hit the air, they get hot enough to glow. We see the larger ones as "falling stars" or "shooting stars." Most meteors burn up before they hit the ground.

Once in a very long while, a big meteor comes along. That's what happened 50,000 years ago.

A huge ball of rock 150 feet across came out of the sky. It was speeding toward our planet at 40,000 miles an hour!

The meteor slammed into the ground with the force of 20 million tons of explosives. It made a huge crater 700 feet deep and 4,000 feet across. It tossed rocks the size of elephants as if they were children's blocks.

The meteor itself was destroyed. Part of it was turned into gas, and much of the rest melted. What was left was broken into tiny particles.

That meteor's "autograph" can still be seen in Arizona. The crater is so big that it could hold 20 football games at once.

If you go to this meteor crater, you can see the deep trough. Rough, rocky ground lies all around it. You can walk on this rim, but it is tough to do. The ground is still piled high with rocks tossed up by the meteor.

As you take your photographs, you may pause and wonder. When will the next large meteor visit us from space? By then, with enough warning, we may be able to send it back!

Think About It

1. What are meteors? When can we see them?

2. How are comets different from meteors?

3. Make a postcard you could send from the meteor crater in Arizona. Draw a picture for one side of the postcard. For the other side, write a message to a friend.